Meditations from
Conversations with God

book 1

Meditations from
Conversations with God

· an uncommon dialogue ·

book 1

Neale Donald Walsch

BERKLEY BOOKS, NEW YORK

A Berkley Book
Published by The Berkley Publishing Group
A division of Penguin Putnam Inc.
375 Hudson Street
New York, New York 10014

Copyright © 1997 by Neale Donald Walsch.
Text design by Irving Perkins Associates.

Published by arrangement with Hampton Roads Publishing Company.
For information address: Hampton Roads Publishing Company, Inc.,
134 Burgess Lane, Charlottesville, Virginia 22902.

PRINTING HISTORY
Berkley trade paperback edition / September 1997

Library of Congress Cataloging-in-Publication Data

Walsch, Neale Donald.
Meditations from Conversations with God.
Book 1 : an uncommon dialogue / Neale Donald Walsch.
[Conversations with God. Selections]—Berkley trade pbk. ed.
New York : Berkley Books, 1997.
p.   cm.
ISBN 978-0-425-16169-2
1. God—Miscellanea.   2. Spritual life—Miscellanea.   3. Meditations.
I. Title.

BL624.2.W342   1997   97204039
291.4'32—dc21

Prologue

When I was a child, my mother used to say, "God is always with you. God is your best friend." Of course, I believed her. She was, after all, my mother. It never occurred to me that she might not be speaking from her own experience. It never occurred to me that my mother may not have felt God's actual presence in *her* everyday life.

But as I grew older, *I* began to have doubts. I never doubted my mother's faith, but I began to wonder about its source. I had never had any direct experience of God in *my* life, and for someone who was "always with me," God was remarkably non-present. I never stopped believing in the existence of God, mind you. I just didn't quite get that God was even aware of—much less interested—in me.

Then in February 1992 I had an experience that changed all that. That was the month in which God began to speak to me. Personally. We entered, in fact, into a rather extensive dialogue. Lasting one full year, our exchanges became a book. We called it *Conversations with God*. Our conversation quenched in me an enormous thirst, satisfied in me an incredible hunger. And I hoped that by sharing it, it could do the same for others.

We have been searching for the God of our heart for a very long time. The God I met in my conversation was not a God to fear, but a God of unconditional and unlimited love. A God of deep compassion and understanding. A God of wonderful humor who takes pure delight in the joyful celebration of life. This is a God offering friendship, not lordship—and asking, in return, for friendship, not worship.

That is the God I would like all of us to know. And the wisdom of that kind God is the wisdom I wish we could live each day. These meditations offer a chance to do just that. Taken from the pages of *Conversations with God*, these words have been very helpful, very meaningful, and very inspiring to me.

I invite you to open this book each morning and embrace the day's thought. Meditate on its meaning. Then seek to bring that meaning into your life as you go about your day. At the close of the day, open this book again, turning to the page with which you began your morning. Read once more the words for the day. Take a moment to reflect on the hours just past, and the new context within which the words may be considered. Then close the book with thanks. And, if it feels good to do so, write in your journal what has come to you from this process. Put down whatever comes to your mind.

In this way you can use the daily meditations here to begin your own conversation with God.

—Neale Donald Walsch
Ashland, Oregon
May 1997

Meditations from
Conversations with God

book 1

January 1

It is not God's function to create or
uncreate the circumstances and
conditions of your life. God
created You, in the image and
likeness of God. You have created
the rest.

p. 13

January 2

Do the deed that you want to have
the new thought about. Then say
the words that you want to have
your new thought about. Do this
often enough and you'll train the
mind to think a new way.

p. 164

January 3

I have always been here to help
you, I am here now. You don't
have to find the answers on your
own. You never had to.

p. 66

January 4

A true Master is not the one with
the most students, but one who
creates the most Masters.

p. 114

January 5

Your ideas about Right and Wrong
are just that—ideas. They are the
thoughts which form the shape
and create the substance of Who
You Are. There would be only one
reason to change any of these;
only one purpose in making an
alteration; if you are not happy
with who you are.

p. 62

January 6

Life is eternal. You are immortal.
You never do die. You simply
change form.

p. 193

January 7

God's greatest moment is the
moment you realize you need no
God.

p. 114

January 8

Let your love propel your beloveds
into the world—and into the full
experience of who they are. In this
will you have truly loved.

p. 115

January 9

If you have caught yourself in an
ungodly act as a result of doing
what is best for you, the confusion
is not in having put yourself first,
but rather in misunderstanding
what is best for you.

p. 132

January 10

Treating others with love does not
necessarily mean allowing others
to do as they wish.

p. 132

January 11

God asks only that you include
yourself among those you love.

p. 132

January 12

If there were such a thing as sin,
this would be it: to allow yourself
to become what you are because
of the experience of others.

p. 62

January 13

If your values serve you, hold to
them. Argue for them. Fight to
defend them. Yet seek to fight in a
way which harms no one. Harm is
not a necessary ingredient in
healing.

p. 62

January 14

The soul—your soul—knows all
there is to know all the time. There
is nothing hidden to it, nothing
unknown. Yet knowing is not
enough. The soul seeks to
experience.

p. 22

January 15

You can know yourself to be
generous, but unless you do
something which displays
generosity, you have nothing but a
concept. You can know yourself to
be kind, but unless you do
someone a kindness, you have
nothing but an idea about yourself.

p. 22

January 16

The first thing to understand about the universe is that no condition is "good" or "bad." It just is. So stop making value judgments.

p. 79

January 17

The first step in changing anything
is to know and accept that you
have chosen it to be what it is. If
you can't accept this on a personal
level, agree to it through your
understanding that we are all one.
Seek then to create change not
because a thing is wrong, but
because it no longer makes an
accurate statement of who you are.

p. 36

January 18

My purpose in creating you, My
spiritual offspring, was for Me to
know Myself as God. I have no
way to do that save through you.

p. 26

January 19

By your decisions you paint a
portrait of Who You Are.

p. 154

January 20

No one who has attained mastery
is dull. Unusual, perhaps.
Extraordinary, perhaps. But never
dull.

p. 78

January 21

Have you ever seen anything more
perfect than a snowflake? Its
intricacy, its design, its symmetry,
its conformity to itself and
originality from all else are all a
mystery. You wonder at the
miracle of this awesome display of
nature. Yet if I can do this with a
single snowflake, what think you I
can do—have done—with the
universe?

p. 43

January 22

I will do nothing for you that you
will not do for your Self. That is
the law and the prophets.

p. 50

January 23

You cannot experience yourself as
what you are until you've
encountered what you are not.
This is the purpose of the theory of
relativity, and all physical life. It is
by that which you are not that you
yourself are defined.

p. 27

January 24

I suggest that it is your judgments
which keep you from joy, and your
expectations which make you
unhappy.

p. 108

January 25

Masters are those who have chosen
only love. In every instance. In
every moment. In every
circumstance.

p. 57

January 26

I invite you to a new form of
communication with God. A two-
way communication. In truth, it is
you who have invited Me. For I
have come to you, in this form,
right now, in answer to your call.

p. 7

January 27

You must first learn to honor and
cherish and love your Self.

p. 126

January 28

Every heart which earnestly asks,
Which is the path to God? is
shown.

p. 94

January 29

The process of prayer becomes
much easier when, rather than
having to believe that God will
always say yes to every request,
one understands intuitively that the
request itself is not necessary.

p. 13

January 30

When you have a thought that is
not in alignment with your higher
vision, change to a new thought,
then and there. When you say a
thing that is out of alignment with
your grandest idea, make a note
not to say something like that
again.

p. 78

January 31

You are goodness and mercy and
compassion and understanding.
You are peace and joy and light.
You are forgiveness and patience,
strength and courage, a helper in
time of need, a comforter in time
of sorrow, a healer in time of
injury, a teacher in times of
confusion.

p. 121

February 1

God is the energy you call
imagination. God is creation. God
is first thought. And God is last
experience. And God is everything
in between.

p. 198

February 2

Your teachers have told you of an
angry God, a jealous God, a God
who needs to be needed. And that
is not a God at all, but a neurotic
substitute for that which would be
a deity.

p. 114

February 3

It is your first nature to be
unconditionally loving.

p. 78

February 4

I will do nothing for you that you
will not do for your Self. That is
the law of the prophets. The world
is in the condition it is in because
of you, and the choices you have
made—or failed to make. The
Earth is in the shape it's in because
of you, and the choices you have
made—or failed to make. Your
own life is the way it is because of
you, and the choices you have
made—or failed to make.

p. 50

February 5

Bless every person and condition,
and give thanks Thus you affirm
the perfection of God's creation—
and show your faith in it. For
nothing happens by accident in
God's world, and there is no such
thing as coincidence. Nor is the
world buffeted by random choice,
or something you call fate!

p. 114

February 6

There is only what serves you, and
what does not. The terms "right"
and "wrong" are relative terms.

p. 162

February 7

Allow each soul to walk its path.

p. 47

February 8

There is nothing scary about life if
you are not attached to results.

p. 110

February 9

You are, have always been and
will always be, a divine part of the
divine whole, a member of the
body. That is why the act of
rejoining the Whole, of returning to
God, is called remembrance. You
actually choose to re-member Who
You Really Are, or to join together
with the various parts of you to
experience the all of you—which
is to say, the All of Me.

p. 28

February 10

Your perception of ultimate reality
is more limited than you thought,
and Truth is more unlimited than
you can imagine.

p. 197

February 11

This is the second great illusion of
man: that the outcome of life is in
doubt. It is this doubt about
ultimate outcome that has created
your greatest enemy, which is fear.
For if you doubt outcome, then
you must doubt the creator—you
must doubt God.

p. 14

February 12

I have given you nothing shameful,
least of all your very body, and its
functions.

p. 208

February 13

Ultimately all Spirit renounces what
is not real, and nothing in the life
you lead is real, save your
relationship with Me.

p. 100

February 14

At the critical juncture in all human
relationships, there is only one
question:
What would love do now?

p. 130

February 15

There are those who say you must
overcome your desires. I say you
must simply change them. The first
practice feels like a rigorous
discipline, the second, a joyful
exercise.

p. 100

February 16

You're setting your sights too low.
Broaden the scope of your
horizons. Extend the depth of your
vision. See more in you than you
think there is to be seen.

p. 142

February 17

You are the deepest wisdom and
the highest truth; the greatest
peace and the grandest love. You
are these things. And in moments
of your life you have known
yourself as these things. Choose
now to know yourself as these
things always.

p. 87

February 18

People assume that if God were to talk directly with you, God would not sound like the fella next door.

p. 68

February 19

Stop making judgments against
yourself.

p. 71

February 20

The world exists the way it exists—
just as a snowflake exists the way
it exists—quite by design. You
have created it that way—just as
you have created your life exactly
as it is.

p. 49

February 21

Your body, your mind and your
soul (spirit) are one. In this, you
are a microcosm of Me—the
Divine All, the Holy Everything,
the Sum and the Substance.

p. 197

February 22

The deepest secret is that life is not
a process of discovery, but a
process of creation. You are not
discovering yourself, but creating
yourself anew. Seek, therefore, not
to find out who you are, seek to
determine who you want to be.

p. 21

February 23

This is the root of every problem
you experience in your life—you
do not consider yourself worthy
enough to be spoken to by God.
Good heavens, how can you ever
expect to hear my voice if you
don't imagine yourself to be
deserving enough to even be
spoken to?

p. 162

February 24

One day, if you have a great deal
of courage, you will experience a
world where making love is
considered better than making war.
On that day will you rejoice.

p. 109

February 25

Life will "take off" for you . . .
when you choose for it to . . . you
must believe the promise and live
it. You must live the promise of
God.

p. 75

February 26

Stop questioning your motives
(you do it incessantly) and let's get
on with it.

p. 70

February 27

You are evolving, you are
becoming. And you are using your
relationship with everything to
decide what you are becoming.
This is the job you came here to
do. This is the joy of creating self.
Of knowing self. Of becoming,
consciously, what you wish to be.

p. 126

February 28

Come to Me along the path of your
heart, not through a journey of
your mind. You will never find Me
in your mind.

p. 94

February 29

Would you not be better off to
think the thoughts you want to
think, than those of others? Are
you not better armed with creative
thoughts than with reactive
thoughts?

p. 165

March 1

You say it is difficult to walk the path of Christ, to follow the teachings of the Buddha, to hold the light of Krishna, to be a Master. Yet I tell you this: It is far more difficult to deny Who You Are than to accept it.

p. 86

March 2

If humans do not change some of
their Sponsoring Thoughts,
humankind could doom itself to
extinction.

p. 164

March 3

Worry is the activity of a mind
which does not understand its
connection with Me.

March 4

No prayer—and a prayer is
nothing more than a fervent
statement of what is so—goes
unanswered.

p. 12

March 5

It is when the going gets tough that
you so often forget Who You Are,
and the tools I have given you for
creating the life that you would
choose.

p. 116

March 6

The job of the soul, of course, is to
cause us to choose the grandeur—
to select the best of who you are—
without condemning that which
you do not select.

p. 84

March 7

If a thing is obviously right, do it.

p. 47

March 8

Envy not success, nor pity failure,
for you know not what is success
or failure in the soul's reckoning.

p. 33

March 9

Relationships are constantly
challenging, constantly calling you
to create, express and experience
higher and higher aspects of
yourself, grander and grander
visions of yourself, ever more
magnificent versions of yourself.

p. 121

March 10

Everlasting perspective helps you
keep things in their proper light.

p. 116

March 11

It's important now, it's time now,
to change your mind about some
things. This is what evolution is all
about.

p. 168

March 12

The person who has the "faith to move mountains," and dies six weeks later, has moved mountains for six weeks. That may have been enough for him.

March 13

There is perfection in the process,
and all life arises out of choice. It is
not appropriate to interfere with
choice, nor to question it. It is
particularly inappropriate to
condemn it.

p. 47

March 14

A society living in fear very often—
actually, inevitably—produces in
form that which it fears most.

p. 55

March 15

Everything in life is holy.

p. 68

March 16

Killing can never be justified as a
means of expressing anger,
releasing hostility, "righting a
wrong" or punishing an offender.

p. 151

March 17

By their decisions your religions
have created lasting, indelible
impressions. By their decisions
your societies have produced their
self-portraits, too. Are you pleased
with these pictures? Are these the
impressions you wish to make?

p. 154

March 18

This is My plan for you. This is My
ideal: that I should become
realized through you.

p. 43

March 19

You must live the promise of God.

p. 75

March 20

You are in a partnership with God.
We share an eternal covenant. My
promise to you is to always give
you what you ask. Your promise is
to ask.

p. 73

March 21

I have established Laws in the
universe that make it possible for
you to have—to create—exactly
what you choose. These Laws
cannot be violated, nor can they be
ignored.

p. 73

March 22

You will never disserve your
relationship—nor anyone—by
seeing more in another than they
are showing you. For there is more
there. Much more. It is only their
fear that stops them from showing
you.

p. 142

March 23

Health will improve almost at once
when worrying ends.

p. 188

March 24

If you think your life is about
doingness, you do not understand
what you are about. Your soul
doesn't care what you do for a
living—and when your life is over,
neither will you. Your soul cares
only about what you're being
while you're doing whatever
you're doing.

p. 170

March 25

The question is not, why start off
on such a path? You have already
started off. You did so with the first
beat of your heart. The question is:
Do I wish to walk this path
consciously, or unconsciously?

p. 156

March 26

So long as you entertain the notion
that there is something or someone
else out there "doing it" to you,
you disempower yourself to do
anything about it.

p. 36

March 27

Do not feel abandoned. I am
always with you.

p. 210

March 28

Desire is the beginning of all
creation. It is first thought. It is a
grand feeling within the soul. It is
God, choosing what next to create.

p. 65

March 29

You don't have a clear focus;
you're not really sure what's true
for you. And the universe is just a
big Xerox machine. It simply
produces multiple copies of your
thoughts. Now there's only one
way to change all that. You have to
change your thought about it.

p. 163

March 30

It might not be a bad goal in your
life to know the highest part of
your Self, and to stay centered in
that.

p. 126

March 31

Expectations ruin relationships.

p. 142

April 1

Do you imagine that God does not
enjoy a good joke? Is it your
knowing that God is without
humor? I tell you, God invented
humor.

p. 60

April 2

Your happy destiny is unavoidable.
You cannot not be "saved." There
is no hell except not knowing this.

p. 115

April 3

The Master knows intuitively that
passion is the path. It is the way to
self-realization. Even in earthly
terms it can be fairly sad that if you
have a passion for nothing, you
have no life at all.

p. 102

April 4

You have no obligation in
relationship. You have only
opportunity. Opportunity, not
obligation, is the cornerstone of
religion, the basis of spirituality. So
long as you see it the other way
around, you will have missed the
point.

p. 137

April 5

You are wont to rush to judgment,
to call a thing "wrong" or "bad" or
"not enough," rather than to bless
what you do not choose.

p. 84

April 6

You are in the process of
experiencing yourself by creating
yourself anew in every single
moment. As am I. Through you.

p. 75

April 7

Sometimes, when a person is really
deeply asleep, you have to shake
him a little.

p. 191

April 8

There is no need to recriminate
yourself. Simply notice what
you've been choosing and choose
again.

April 9

Every prayer—every thought,
every feeling, every statement—is
creative. To the extent that it is
fervently held as truth, to that
degree will it be made manifest in
your experience.

p. 12

April 10

You can choose to be a person
who has resulted simply from what
has happened, or from what you
have chosen to be and do about
what has happened.

p. 122

April 11

Call not a thing calamity, nor
joyous event, until you decide, or
witness, how it is used.

p. 33

April 12

Your soul seeks the highest
feeling. It seeks to experience—to
be—perfect love.

p. 85

April 13

The reason that the true Master
does not complain is that the true
Master is not suffering, but simply
experiencing a set of circumstances
that you *would call insufferable.*

p. 107

April 14

You have nothing to learn about
relationships. You have only to
demonstrate what you already
know.

p. 121

April 15

True Masters are those who have
chosen to make a life, rather than a
living.

p. 176

April 16

God is in the sadness and in
laughter. In the bitter and the
sweet.

p. 60

April 17

There are those who say that to
know God you must overcome all
earthly passions. Yet to understand
and accept them is enough. What
you resist persists. What you look
at disappears.

p. 100

April 18

I will not leave you, I cannot leave
you, for you are My creation and
My product, My daughter and My
son, My purpose and My . . . Self.
Call on me, therefore, wherever
and whenever you are separate
from the peace that I am.

p. 211

April 19

Fear is the opposite of everything
you are.

p. 188

April 20

You cannot lie to yourself. Your
mind knows the truth of your
thoughts.

p. 11

April 21

This is both the goal and the glory
of God: that His subjects shall be
no more, and that all shall know
God not as the unattainable, but as
the unavoidable.

p. 115

April 22

When you achieve certain states of
being over a long period of time,
success in what you are doing in
the world is very difficult to avoid.

p. 176

April 23

There is no such thing as karmic
debt.

p. 204

April 24

Sex is an extraordinary expression
of love—love of another, love of
self, love of life. You ought to
therefore love it!

p. 208

April 25

Do not dismantle the house, but
look at each brick, and replace
those which appear broken, which
no longer support the structure.

p. 62

April 26

In the moment of your total
knowing, you, too, will feel as I do
always: totally joyful, loving,
accepting, blessing and grateful.
These are the Five Attitudes of
God.

p. 65

April 27

Only when you say "I did this" can
you find the power to change it.

p. 36

April 28

You have a right to your joy; Seek
it! Find it!

p. 186

April 29

Are you not being allowed to
experience everything? The tears,
the joy, the pain, the gladness, the
exaltation, the massive depression,
the win, the lose, the draw? What
more is there?

p. 158

April 30

My teachers have all come with the
same message. Not "I am holier
than thou," but "you are as holy as
am I."

p. 127

May 1

The purpose of relationship is not
to have another who might
complete you; but to have another
with whom you might share your
completeness.

p. 123

May 2

Your world would not be in its
present condition were you to
have simply listened to your
experience. The result of your not
listening to your experience is that
you keep reliving it, over and over
again.

p. 5

May 3

If you think you are right about
everything, who needs to talk with
God?

p. 7

May 4

Why not simply acknowledge the
truth when you hear it, and move
towards it?

p. 119

May 5

My messages will come in a
hundred forms, at a thousand
moments, across a million years.
You cannot miss them if you truly
listen. You cannot ignore them
once truly heard.

p. 6

May 6

There is a divine purpose behind
everything, and therefore a divine
presence in everything.

p. 60

May 7

Some people don't like to be
awakened. Most do not. Most
would rather sleep.

p. 191

May 8

You can't go wrong. It's not part of
the plan. There's no way not to get
where you are going. There's no
way to miss your destination. If
God is your target, you're in luck,
because God is so big, you can't
miss.

p. 88

May 9

Do not condemn, therefore, all that
you would call bad in the world.
Rather, ask yourself, what about
this have you judged bad, and
what, if anything, you wish to do
to change it.

p. 32

May 10

If you are God's equal, that means
nothing is being done to you—and
all things are created by you. There
can be no more victims and no
more villians—only outcomes of
your thought about a thing.

p. 75

May 11

Your will for you is God's will for you.

p. 13

May 12

Each circumstance is a gift, and in
each experience is hidden a
treasure.

p. 33

May 13

Love is the ultimate reality. It is the
only. The all. The feeling of love is
your experience of God.

p. 56

May 14

Do you want your life to truly take
off? Then change your idea about
it. About you. Think, speak and act
as the God you are.

p. 76

May 15

Listen to me in the truth of your
soul. Listen to me in the feelings of
your heart. Listen to me in the
quiet of your mind.

p. 210

May 16

Well, if God can't inspire you, who in hell can?

p. 88

May 17

I have never set down a "right" or "wrong," a "do" or a "don't." To do so would be to strip you completely of your greatest gift— the opportunity to do as you please, and experience the results of that.

p. 39

May 18

We dare not solve all the
problems, or there will be nothing
left for us to do.

May 19

Go first to your Highest Thought
about yourself. Imagine the you
that you would be if you lived that
thought every day.

p. 77

May 20

Judge not, and neither condemn,
for you know not why a thing
occurs, nor to what end.

p. 38

May 21

The work of the soul is to wake
yourself up. The work of God is to
wake everybody else up.

p. 142

May 22

If you choose evolution—the
evolution of your soul—you won't
produce that by the worldy
activities of your body.

p. 170

May 23

For goodness' sake, don't destroy
sexual innocence and pleasure and
the purity of the fun, the joy, by
misusing sex. Don't use it for
power or hidden purpose; for ego
gratification or domination; or any
purpose other than the purest joy
and the highest ecstasy, given and
shared—which is love.

p. 206

May 24

You are the creator of your reality,
and life can show up no other way
for you than that way in which you
think it will.

p. 52

May 25

There is nothing you cannot be.
There is nothing you cannot do.
There is nothing you cannot have.
What other kind of promise would
you have God make? Would you
believe Me if I promised you less?

p. 44

May 26

When you choose the action love
sponsors, then will you do more
than survive, then will you do
more than win, then will you do
more than succeed. Then will
you experience the full glory of
Who You Really Are, and who you
can be.

p. 19

May 27

Do Me a favor and don't try to
contain Me. By the way, do
yourself the same favor.

p. 88

May 28

You have come here to work out
an individual plan for your own
salvation. Yet salvation does not
mean saving yourself from the
snares of the devil. There is no
such thing as the devil, and hell
does not exist. You are saving
yourself from the oblivion of non-
realization.

p. 51

May 29

Every one of My messengers has
been defiled. Far from gaining
glory, they have gained nothing
but heartache. Are you willing?
Does your heart ache to tell the
truth about Me?

p. 145

May 30

I gave to each of the countless
parts of Me (to all of my spirit
children) the same power to create
which I have as the whole.

p. 25

May 31

It is your first nature to be
unconditionally loving. It is your
second nature to choose to express
your first nature, your true nature,
consciously.

p. 78

June 1

Words are merely utterances:
noises that stand for feelings,
thoughts and experience. They are
symbols. Signs. Insignias. They are
not Truth. They are not the real
thing.

p. 4

June 2

Most people enter into
relationships with an eye toward
what they can get out of them,
rather than what they can put into
them.

p. 122

June 3

Feeling guilty is a learned
response.

p. 119

June 4

Fear is the other end of love. It is
the primal polarity.

p. 57

June 5

If you believe that God is some
omnipotent Being who hears all
prayers, says "yes" to some, "no"
to others, and "maybe, but not
now" to the rest, you are mistaken.
By what rule of thumb would God
decide?

p. 13

June 6

I do not communicate by words
alone. In fact, rarely do I do so. My
most common form of
communication is through feeling.

p. 3

June 7

The world is in the condition it's in
because the world is full of
sleepwalkers.

p. 191

June 8

I will bring you the exact right
thoughts, words or feelings, at any
given moment, suited precisely to
the purpose at hand.

p. 6

June 9

I tell you this: you are your own
rule-maker. You set the guidelines.
And you decide how well you
have done; how well you are
doing.

p. 41

June 10

When you thank God in advance
for that which you choose to
experience in your reality, you, in
effect, acknowledge that it is there.

p. 11

June 11

Your first relationship must be with yourself.

p. 126

June 12

For thousands of years people
have disbelieved the promises of
God for the most extraordinary
reason: they were too good to be
true.

p. 44

June 13

Begin at once to imagine life the
way you want it to be—and move
into that. Check every thought,
word and action that does not fall
into harmony with that. Move
away from those.

p. 78

June 14

All human actions are motivated at
their deepest level by one of two
emotions—fear or love.

p. 15

June 15

It is not a question of learning, but of remembering.

p. 43

June 16

You can define present conditions
and circumstances as what they
truly are: temporary and temporal.

p. 116

June 17

I want for you what you want for you. Nothing more, nothing less. I don't sit here and make a judgment, request by request, whether something should be granted you. My law is the law of cause and effect, not the law of "We'll See."

June 18

From the highest mountain it has
been shouted, in the lowest pure
its whisper has been heard.
Through the corridors of all human
experience has this Truth been
echoed: Love is the answer.

p. 58

June 19

Worry is just about the worst form
of mental activity there is . . . Worry
is pointless. It is wasted mental
energy.

p. 188

June 20

It is not in the action of another,
but in your re-action, that your
salvation will be found.

p. 127

June 21

I will speak to you if you will
listen. I will come to you if you
will invite Me. I will show you then
that I have always been there. All
ways.

p. 58

June 22

I tell you, you can speak to Me as
you would speak with your best
friend.

p. 60

June 23

Not to decide is to decide.

p. 50

June 24

Marriage is a sacrament. But not
because of its sacred obligations.
Rather, because of its unequaled
opportunity.

p. 138

June 25

The world will need many voices
to speak the words of truth and
healing for which millions long.
The world will need many hearts
joined together in the work of the
soul, and prepared to do the work
of God. Can you honestly claim
that you are not aware of this?

p. 144

June 26

Hear Me, everywhere. Whenever
you have a question, simply know
that I have answered it already.
Then open your eyes to your
world.

p. 210

June 27

There are no coincidences in the
universe.

p. 58

June 28

All conditions are temporary.

p. 79

June 29

So what is your intention now? Do
you intend to prove your theory
that life seldom brings you what
you choose? Or do you intend to
demonstrate Who You Are and
Who I Am?

p. 119

June 30

I tell you there is no such
experience after death as you have
constructed in your fear-based
theologies.

p. 41

July 1

I do not make a judgment about
the creations that you conjure. I
simply empower you to conjure
more—and more and more and
more.

p. 118

July 2

Your saying you want a thing only
works to produce that precise
experience—wanting—in your
reality. The correct prayer is
therefore never a prayer of
supplication, but a prayer of
gratitude.

p. 11

July 3

Are you going to be in a place
called fear, or in a place called
love? Where are you—and where
are you coming from—as you
encounter life?

p. 172

July 4

How can you be a creative being if
I am dictating what you shall be,
do and have? My joy is in your
freedom, not your compliance.

July 5

When life is lived from a
standpoint of damage control or
optimum advantage, the true
benefit of life is forfeited. The
opportunity is lost. The chance is
missed. For a life lived thusly is a
life lived from fear.

p. 130

July 6

Do you not see that I could just as
easily work through your
imagination as anything else?

p. 6

July 7

Obedience is not creation, and
thus can never produce salvation.
Obedience is a response, while
creation is pure choice, undictated,
unrequired.

p. 175

July 8

When you are in your God space,
you know and understand that all
you are now experiencing is
temporary. I tell you that heaven
and earth shall pass away, but you
shall not.

p. 116

July 9

Bring to the space of your
experience the highest and best
idea you ever had about you.

July 10

Mine is always your Highest
Thought, your Clearest Word, your
Grandest Feeling. Anything less is
from another source.

p. 4

July 11

I have heard the crying of your
heart. I have seen the searching of
your soul.

p. 58

July 12

No one will judge you ever, for
why, and how, could God judge
God's own creation and call it bad?

p. 41

July 13

You have brought your Self to the
relative world so that you might
have the tools with which to know
and experience Who You Really
Are. Who You Are is who you
create yourself to be in relationship
to all the rest of it.

p. 126

July 14

Thoughts rooted in fear will
produce one kind of manifestation
on the physical plane, thoughts
rooted in love will produce
another. The masters are those
who have chosen only love. In
every instant. In every moment. In
every circumstance.

p. 57

July 15

Nothing happens to you or
through you that is not for your
own highest good.

p. 174

July 16

Belief in God produces belief in
God's greatest gift—unconditional
love—and God's greatest promise—
unlimited potential.

p. 44

July 17

There are a million aspects to Me.
A billion. A trillion. You see? There
is the profane and the profound,
the lesser and the larger, the
hollow and the holy, the ghastly
and the Godly.

p. 173

July 18

This is the goal of your soul, this is
its purpose: to fully realize itself
while in the body; to become the
embodiment of all that it really is.

p. 43

July 19

Do not what you are obliged to do,
but what you have an opportunity
to do.

p. 145

July 20

The soul leads you to the right and perfect opportunities for you to experience exactly what you had planned to experience. What you actually experience is up to you.

p. 174

July 21

Fear is the energy which contracts,
closes down, draws in, runs, hides,
hoards, harms. Love is the energy
which expands, opens up, sends
out, stays, reveals, shares, heals.

p. 19

July 22

The people who make a living
doing what they love are the
people who insist on doing so.

p. 169

July 23

Suffering has nothing to do with
events, but with one's reaction to
them. What's happening is merely
what's happening. How you feel
about it is another matter.

p. 105

July 24

The actions of the body were
meant to be reflections of a state of
being, not attempts to attain a state
of being.

p. 185

July 25

The way to reduce the pain which
you associate with earthly
experiences and events—both
yours and those of others—is to
change the way you behold them.
You cannot change the outer
event, so you must change the
inner experience.

p. 3

July 26

We make real that to which we
pay attention.

p. 107

July 27

Do you imagine this is too big a
problem for Me to solve? I see, so
it's a matter of faith. You don't
question My ability, you merely
doubt My desire.

p. 117

July 28

The voice within is the loudest
voice with which I speak, because
it is the closest to you. It is the
voice which tells you whether
everything else is true or false,
right or wrong, good or bad as you
have defined it. It is the radar that
sets the course, steers the ship,
guides the journey if you but let it.

p. 20

July 29

The purpose of a relationship is to decide what part of yourself you'd like to see "show up," not what part of another you can capture and hold.

p. 122

July 30

When you have a thought that is
not in alignment with your higher
vision, change to a new thought,
then and there. When you say a
thing which is out of alignment
with your grandest idea, make a
note not to say something like that
again. When you do a thing which
is misaligned with your best
intention, decide to make that the
last time.

p. 78

July 31

What your body is doing is a reflection of what your life is about.

August 1

You are not on this planet to
produce anything with your body.
You on are on this planet to
produce something with your soul.
Your body is simply and merely
the tool of your soul.

p. 172

August 2

The more you are, the more you
can become, and the more you can
become, the more you can yet be.

p. 20

August 3

If you want to know what's true for
you about something, look to how
you're feeling about it. Feelings are
sometimes difficult to discover—
and often even more difficult to
acknowledge. Yet hidden in your
deepest feelings is your highest
truth.

p. 3

August 4

You'll get as many chances as you want and need. You can come back again and again and again. If you do get to the next step, if you evolve to the next level, it's because you want to, not because you have to.

p. 149

August 5

I will continue sending you the
same messages over and over
again, throughout the millenia and
to whatever corner of the universe
you occupy. Endlessly will I send
you My messages, until you have
received them and held them
close, calling them your own.

August 6

It takes great courage to announce
oneself as a man of God. You
understand, the world will much
more readily accept you as
virtually anything else.

p. 145

August 7

Next time, decide to act before you think.

p. 168

August 8

In the true order of things one
does not do something in order to
be happy—one is happy, and,
hence, does something.

p. 185

August 9

Do you think there is a word I
have not heard? A sight I have not
seen? A sound I do not know? Is it
your thought that I despise some
of these, while I love the others? I
tell you, I despise nothing. None of
it is repulsive to Me. It is life, and
life is the gift; the unspeakable
treasure; the holy of holies.

p. 60

August 10

All the "bad" things that happen
are of your choosing. The mistake
is not in choosing them, but in
calling them bad.

p. 36

August 11

The function of the soul is to
indicate its desire, not impose it.

p. 175

August 12

Your life work is a statement of
Who You Are. If it is not, then why
are you doing it?

p. 186

August 13

You cannot experience yourself as
what you are until you've
encountered what you are not.

p. 27

August 14

Seek to change those things—or
support others who are changing
those things—which no longer
reflect your highest sense of Who
You are.

p. 38

August 15

Doing is a function of the body.
Being is a function of the soul.

p. 170

August 16

If you don't like what you've just
created, choose again. My job, as
God, is to always give you that
opportunity.

p. 118

August 17

There is only one purpose for all
of life, and that is for you and all
that lives to experience fullest
glory. Everything else you say,
think or do is attendant to that
function.

p. 20

August 18

If you want guarantees in life, then
you don't want life. You want
rehearsals for a script that's already
been written.

p. 141

August 19

There is no coincidence, and
nothing happens "by accident."

p. 52

August 20

You misunderstand your power. I
tell you this: Your life proceeds out
of your intentions for it.

p. 118

August 21

The soul conceives, the mind
creates, the body experiences. The
circle is complete. The soul then
knows itself in its own experience.

p. 196

August 22

There's a difference between being
and doing, and most people have
placed their emphasis on the latter.

p. 196

August 23

Now, having seen the differences
between where you are and where
you want to be, begin to change—
consciously change—your
thoughts, words and actions to
match your grandest vision.

p. 77

August 24

Move into communion with the
souls of others, and their purpose,
their intention, will be clear to you.

p. 47

August 25

The moral codes, religious
constrictions, social taboos and
emotional conventions you have
placed around sex have made it
virtually impossible for you to
celebrate your being.

p. 208

August 26

You may think this is easy, this Be
Who You Really Are business, but
it's the most challenging thing
you'll ever do in your life.

p. 148

August 27

There is only one reason to do
anything: as a statement to the
universe of Who You Are.

p. 36

August 28

Remember to exercise extreme
judgment regarding what you call
"right" and "wrong."

p. 47

August 29

Are you willing to endure the
ridicule of your fellow human
beings? Are you prepared to give
up glory on Earth for the greater
glory of the soul fully realized?

p. 145

August 30

The spirit in you seeks that grand
moment when you have conscious
awareness of its wishes, and join in
joyful oneness with them.

p. 174

August 31

You are not discovering yourself,
but creating yourself anew. Seek,
therefore, not to find out who you
are, seek to determine who you
want to be.

p. 20

September 1

You call a life of complete freedom "spiritual anarchy." I call it God's great promise. It is only within the context of this promise that God's great plan can be completed.

p. 137

September 2

If, then, revelation is requested, it
cannot be had, for the act of asking
is a statement that it is not there.

p. 10

September 3

The act of resisting something is
the act of granting it life. . . . the
more you resist, the more you
make it real—whatever it is you
are resisting.

p. 102

September 4

You cannot disembark from the
journey. You embarked before you
were born. Your birth is simply a
sign that the journey has begun.

p. 156

September 5

The Highest Thought is always that
thought which contains joy. The
Clearest Words are those words
which contain truth. The Grandest
Feeling is that feeling which you
call love.

September 6

All people are special, and all
moments are golden. There is no
person, and there is no time one
more special than another.

p. 6

September 7

You always get what you create,
and you are always creating.

p. 118

September 8

You cannot know God until you
stop telling yourself that you
already know God. You cannot
hear God until you stop thinking
that you've already heard God.

September 9

If you knew Who You Are—that
you are the most magnificent, the
most remarkable, the most
splendid being God has ever
created—you would never fear.
For who could reject such
wondrous magnificence?

p. 16

September 10

When the body, mind and soul
create together, in harmony and in
unity, God is made flesh. Then
does the soul know itself in its
own experience. Then do the
heavens rejoice.

p. 175

September 11

Judge not that about which you
feel passionate. Simply notice it,
then see if it serves you, given who
and what you wish to be.

p. 100

September 12

Admit honestly to yourself and to
another exactly how you are
feeling.

p. 128

September 13

Inquire within, rather than without, asking: "What part of my Self do I wish to experience now in the face of this calamity? What aspect of being do I choose to call forth?"

p. 32

September 14

You have forgotten what it was
like to be loved without condition.
You do not remember the
experience of the love of God. And
so you try to imagine what God's
love must be like, based on what
you see of love in the world.

p. 17

September 15

The intention is for you not to fail.

p. 149

September 16

Some events you produce willfully, and some events you draw to you— more or less unconsciously. Some events are written off to "fate." Yet even "fate" can be an acronym for "from all thoughts everywhere." In other words, the consciousness of the planet.

p. 106

September 17

The answer is the answer you
cannot hear—for it leaves you
without guidelines and renders null
and void every agreement in the
moment you make it. The answer
is: You have no obligation. Neither
in relationship, nor in all of life.

p. 135

September 18

Seek not to make of your love a
glue that binds, but rather a
magnet that first attracts, then turns
around and repels, lest those who
are attracted begin to believe they
must stick to you to survive.

p. 115

September 19

I have created you—blessed you—
in the image and likeness of Me.

p. 95

September 20

The most difficult thing for people
to do is to hear their own soul.
(Notice that so few people do.)

p. 81

September 21

Sex is joy, and many of you have
made sex everything else but.

p. 207

September 22

You create, collectively and
individually, the life and times you
are experiencing, for the soul
purpose of evolving.

p. 37

September 23

That which you fear strongly you
will experience.

p. 54

September 24

I truly want what you truly want—
nothing different and nothing
more. Don't you see that is my
greatest gift to you?

p. 166

September 25

See the Divine in a baby who
needs changing at 3 a.m. . . . in a
bill that needs paying by the first of
the month. Recognize the hand of
God in the illness that takes a
spouse, the job that's lost, the
child's fever, the parent's pain.
Now we are talking saintliness.

p. 115

September 26

If, now, there is something you
choose to experience in your life,
do not "want it"—choose it.

p. 180

September 27

You are already a God. You simply
do not know it.

p. 202

September 28

Choosing to be God-like does not
mean that you choose to be a
martyr. And it certainly does not
mean you choose to be a victim.

p. 134

September 29

You cannot create a thing—not a
thought, an object, an event—no
experience of any kind—which is
outside of God's plan.

p. 61

September 30

I understand your fatigue. I know
you are tired of the struggle. Yet I
tell you this: When you follow Me
the struggle disappears.

p. 115

October 1

You can choose to be a person
who has resulted simply from what
has happened, or from what
you've chosen to be and do about
what has happened.

p. 122

October 2

You cannot be ill without at some
level causing yourself to be, and
you can be well again in a moment
by simply deciding to be.

p. 32

October 3

In the moment you pledge your
highest love, you greet your
greatest fear.

p. 16

October 4

I talk to everyone. All the time. The question is not to whom do I talk, but who listens?

p. 3

October 5

Listen to your feelings. Listen to
your highest thoughts. Listen to
your experience. Whenever any of
these differ from what you've been
told by your teachers, or read in
your books, forget the words.
Words are the least reliable
purveyor of Truth.

p. 8

October 6

It is your soul's only desire to turn
its grandest concept about itself
into its greatest experience.

p. 22

October 7

By that which you call evil do you
define yourself—and by that which
you call good. The biggest evil
would therefore be to declare
nothing evil at all.

p. 134

October 8

When human love relationships
fail, they fail because they were
entered into for the wrong reason.

p. 122

October 9

A Master blesses calamity, for the
Master knows that from the seeds
of disaster (and all experience)
comes the growth of Self. And the
Master's . . . life purpose is always
growth.

p. 129

October 10

Life may more than once call upon
you to prove Who You Are by
demonstrating an aspect of Who
You Are Not.

p. 133

October 11

All of you are special.

p. 143

October 12

You must honor your feelings. For
honoring your feelings means
honoring your Self.

p. 128

October 13

A practicing Master does not speak
of suffering simply because a
Master practicing clearly
understands the power of the
Word—and so chooses to simply
not say a word about it.

p. 107

October 14

The soul is very clear that its
purpose is evolution. That is its
sole purpose—and its soul
purpose. It is not concerned with
the achievements of the body or
the development of the mind.
These are all meaningless to the
soul.

p. 82

October 15

Be watchful of the choices of
others, but not judgmental. Know
that their choice is perfect for them
in this moment now—yet stand
ready to assist them should the
moment come when they seek a
newer choice, a different choice—
a higher choice.

p. 47

October 16

You cannot move away from
something, because it will chase
you all over hell and back.
Therefore, resist not temptation—
but simply turn from it.

p. 104

October 17

You are a three-fold being. You
consist of body, mind and spirit.
You could also call these the
physical, the nonphysical and the
metaphysical. This is the Holy
Trinity, and it has been called by
many names.

p. 73

October 18

The truth is relentless. It won't
leave you alone. It keeps creeping
up on you from every side,
showing you what's really so.

p. 140

October 19

If you do not go within, you go
without.

October 20

It is a great challenge, this path of the householder. There are many distractions, many worldly concerns. The aesthetic is bothered by none of these. He is brought his bread and water, and given his humble mat on which to lie, and he can devote his every hour to prayer, meditation and contemplation of the divine. How easy to see the divine under such circumstances! How simple a task! Ah, but give one a spouse and children!

October 21

Some of you are walking in
wakefulness, and some of you are
sleepwalking. Yet all of you are
creating your own reality—
creating, not discovering.

p. 92

October 22

I have given you the tools with
which to respond and react to
events in a way which reduces—in
fact, eliminates—pain, but you
have not used them.

p. 105

October 23

Look to your experience to find
your truth.

p. 109

October 24

The point of life is not to get
anywhere—it is to notice that you
are, and have always been, already
there.

p. 104

October 25

The Laws are very simple.

1. Thought is creative.

2. Fear attracts like energy.

3. Love is all there is.

p. 56

October 26

There is no such thing as an
incorrect path—for on this journey
you cannot "not get" where you
are going. It is simply a matter of
speed—merely a question of when
you will get there.

p. 104

October 27

The word of God was not a
commandment, but a covenant.

p. 95

October 28

What you open your eyes and look
at disappears. That is, it ceases to
hold its illusory form.

p. 102

October 29

All of your life you think you are
your body. Some of the time you
think you are your mind. It is at
the time of your death that you
find out Who You Really Are.

p. 81

October 30

The grandest teaching of Christ
was not that you shall have
everlasting life—but that you do.

p. 52

October 31

A true leader is not the one with
the most followers, but one who
creates the most leaders.

p. 114

November 1

The realm of the relative was
created in order that I might
experience My Self. This does not
make the realm of the relative real.
It is a created reality you and I
have devised.

p. 56

November 2

If you cannot depend upon God's
love to always be there, on whose
love can you depend?

p. 16

November 3

Feeling is the language of the soul.

p. 3

November 4

What you fear most is what will
most plague you. Fear will draw it
to you like a magnet.

p. 56

November 5

Joy, truth, love. These three are
interchangeable, and one always
leads to the other. It matters not in
which order they are placed.

p. 5

November 6

My purpose will not be thwarted,
nor My will be ignored. You will
get the message. Sooner or later.

p. 5

November 7

What you resist persists.

p. 102

November 8

Do you imagine that a human soul
encounters life challenges—
whatever they may be—by
accident? Is this your imagining?

p. 45

November 9

Many people choose to believe
that God communicates in special
ways and only with special people.
This removes the mass of the
people from responsibility for
hearing My message . . . and allows
them to take someone else's word
for everything.

p. 6

November 10

The original wisdom surrounding
suffering in silence has become so
perverted that now many believe
(and several religions actually
teach) that suffering is good, and
joy is bad.

p. 108

November 11

Words may help you understand
something. Experience allows you
to know.

p. 4

November 12

Nothing stays the same, nothing
remains static. Which way a thing
changes depends on you.

p. 79

November 13

From the beginning all man has
ever wanted is to love and be
loved. And from the beginning of
time man has done everything in
his power to make it impossible to
do that.

p. 208

November 14

You cannot be what you do not
know your Self to be.

p. 201

November 15

You are telling me that you haven't
always gotten what you wanted.
Yet I am here to tell you that
you've always gotten what you
called forth. Your life is always a
result of your thoughts about it.

p. 118

November 16

You may do as you wish without
fear of retribution. It may serve
you, however, to be aware of
consequences. Consequences are
results. Natural outcomes. These
are not at all the same as
retributions or punishments.

p. 42

November 17

This is the greatest barrier to your
enlightenment: You think you
already know the truth! You think
you already understand how it is.
So you agree with everything that
falls into the paradigm of your
understanding, and reject
everything which does not. And
this you call learning.

p. 195

November 18

Nothing occurs in your life—
nothing—which is not first a
thought. Thoughts are like
magnets, drawing effects to you.

p. 188

November 19

Everyone can love everything the
moment they understand what
they are doing, and why.

p. 186

November 20

A true teacher is not the one with
the most knowledge, but one who
causes the most others to have
knowledge.

p. 115

November 21

How can you think of wasting a
moment doing something for a
living you don't like to do? What
kind of a living is that? That is not
a living, that is a dying!

p. 185

November 22

Each to his own, without judgment—
that is the motto.

p. 206

November 23

Begin by being still. Quiet the
outer world, so that the inner
world might bring you sight.

p. 44

November 24

There is nothing you can't have if
you choose it. Even before you
ask, I will have given it to you.

p. 117

November 25

When body, mind and soul create
together, in harmony and in unity,
God is made flesh. Then does the
soul know itself in its own
experience. Then do the heavens
rejoice.

p. 175

November 26

The Holy Spirit will not force His
will upon your soul. It is outside of
the nature of the spirit to do so,
and thus, quite literally, impossible.

p. 175

November 27

Keep on deciding what you want
to become in the next highest
version of your Self. Keep on
working toward that. This is God
Work we're up to, You and I, so
keep on!

p. 158

November 28

There is no limit to what you can
become.

p. 201

November 29

There are those who say that I
have given you free will, yet these
same people claim that if you do
not obey Me, I will send you to
hell. What kind of free will is that?

p. 39

November 30

Now is the time to go to your God
space more than ever.

p. 116

December 1

If the entity which is you is to
create, and thus know, who it
really is, it must be through an act
of conscious volition, not an act of
unconscious obedience.

p. 175

December 2

Thankfulness is the most powerful
statement to God; an affirmation
that even before you ask, I have
answered. Therefore, never
supplicate, appreciate.

p. 11

December 3

I tell you this: I am performing a
miracle right now.

p. 69

December 4

Every human thought, and every
human action, is based in either
love or fear. There is no other
human motivation.

p. 15

December 5

Be patient. You are gaining
wisdom.

p. 158

December 6

I have given you a free will—the
power to do as you choose—and I
will never take that away from you,
ever.

p. 5

December 7

Go ahead and do what you really
love to do! Do nothing else!

p. 185

December 8

All of your holy scriptures—of every religious persuasion and tradition—contain the clear admonition: Fear not. Do you think this is by accident?

p. 54

December 9

Life's irony is that as soon as world
goods and world success are of no
concern to you, the way is open
for them to flow to you.

p. 176

December 10

Are you going to be in a place
called fear, or in a place called
love? Where are you—and where
are you coming from—as you
encounter life?

p. 172

December 11

Turn toward Me and away from
anything unlike Me.

p. 104

December 12

Bless every person and condition,
and give thanks. Thus you affirm
the perfection of God's creation—
and show your faith in it.

p. 46

December 13

Ultimately all Spirit renounces what
is not real, and nothing in the life
you lead is real, save your
relationship with Me.

p. 100

December 14

The First Law is that you can be,
do and have whatever you can
imagine. The Second Law is that
you attract what you fear.

p. 54

December 15

Suffering has nothing to do with
events, but with one's reaction to
them.

p. 105

December 16

The soul's decision precedes the
body's action in a highly conscious
person.

p. 185

December 17

In seeking to be Me, the soul has a
grand job ahead of it; an enormous
menu of beingness from which to
choose. And that is what it is doing
in this moment now.

p. 173

December 18

Religion is your attempt to speak
of the unspeakable. It does not do
a very good job.

p. 195

December 19

Nothing holy has ever been
achieved through denial. Yet
desires change as even larger
realities are glimpsed.

p. 206

December 20

What you actually experience is up
to you. It could be what you
planned to experience, or it could
be something else, depending
upon what you choose.

p. 174

December 21

You have this idea that God shows
up in only one way in life. That's a
very dangerous idea. It stops you
from seeing God all over.

p. 59

December 22

If a snowflake is utterly perfect in
its design, do you not think the
same could be said about
something as magnificent as your
life?

p. 46

December 23

No one does anything he doesn't
want to do.

p. 186

December 24

You are peace and joy and light.

p. 86

December 25

I have come to you, in this form,
right now, in answer to your call.

p. 7

December 26

The supreme irony here is that you
have all placed so much
importance on the Word of God,
and so little on the experience.

p. 4

December 27

You are, always and forever, in the
moment of pure creation.

p. 104

December 28

Joy and sacredness do mix (they
are, in fact, the same thing), and
many of you think that they do
not.

p. 207

December 29

You must first see yourself as
worthy before you can see another
as worthy. You must first see
yourself as blessed before you can
see another as blessed. You must
first know your Self to be holy
before you can acknowledge
holiness in another.

December 30

My Truth—and your surest help in
time of need—is as awesome as
the night sky, and as simply,
incontrovertibly, trustful as a baby's
gurgle. It is as loud as a pounding
heartbeat—and as quiet as a breath
taken in unity with Me.

p. 210

December 31

You want bells and whistles? I'll
see what I can arrange.

p. 59

About the Artist

Louis Jones is a native of Tidewater, Virginia. His egg temperas, watercolors, and drawings reflect his love of nature and his love for people—capturing, as he describes, "the moving skies, the fluid landscapes, the hopes and dreams of all people, the heart and soul of humanity." Jones's work has been shown in galleries and museums throughout the United States and Europe, and he was one of the select American artists to display at the Contemporary Art Exhibit in Bath, England. He has also been included in *American Artists of Renown.*

For a limited edition of the original cover painting, *New Dawn,* by Louis Jones, please contact:

The Louis & Susan Jones Art Gallery
Dominion Tower, Suite 105
999 Waterside Drive
Norfolk, VA 23510

Phone: (757) 625-6505
Fax: (757) 499-5586
for further information